possible initial consonants. Book 6 deals with the double initial consonant, as *'br'* in *bridge*. Some of these can be 'built' from the sounds of the two letters, but it is far better for children to learn them as one combined sound. Often, sounds such as 'sh' in *ship* and 'ch' in *chop* cannot be built anyway. The initial consonants plus vowel often represent the first vital syllable in any word.

The books show one main word, with its full-colour illustration, together with clues to additional words, in line only, at the foot of the page. Extra words using the same sounds are given for reference and conversation. Parents and teachers should emphasise the combined effect of consonant and vowel, making possible the reading of the whole first syllable. This will prove a great aid to children tackling new words in later reading. If the illustration does not provide sufficient clue, the full starting sound of consonant plus vowel should be given.

Recognising individual letters is essential if the full value of phonic training is to be obtained, so it is important for children to *write* the letters at the same time as learning to say them. Writing practice reinforces memory, a vital part of a child's learning process.

sounds and pictures
BOOK 2

by MERVYN BENFORD
illustrated by GERALD WITCOMB

Ladybird Books Ltd Loughborough 1976

eg

egg

more words to say
ever, every, errand, empty

You may see him at the Zoo.

be

belt

more words to say
berry, best, bend, bet, better, beg

What are these?

ce

centipede

more words to say
centre, century, centimetre

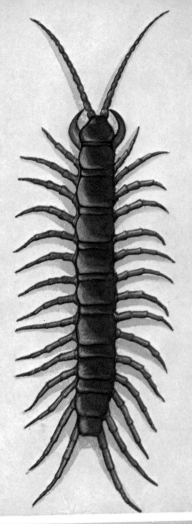

Naughty men and women
may have to live in one of these.

de

desk

more words to say
den, devil, desert, dent, deck

He checks up on your teeth.

fe

fence

more words to say
ferry, fell, fellow, fed, fetch

This month sometimes
has 29 days.

FEBRUARY

S	··	··	2	9	16	23
M	··	··	3	10	17	24
T	··	··	4	11	18	25
W	··	··	5	12	19	26

he

helmet

more words to say
help, hedgehog, heron

Has the — — — come through the — — — — — ?

je

jet

more words to say
jetty, jest

Do you like this for tea ?

ke

kettle

more words to say
keg, kestrel, ketchup

Has the dog run away
from his −−−−−− ?

le

lemon

more words to say
ledge, lettuce, let, lend, left, less,
length, level

What are these?

me

melon

more words to say
metal, message, melt, mend, men,
mess, metric

Men and women are given these for being brave.

ne

nest

more words to say
neck, next, nettle, never, necessary

You could catch fish in this!

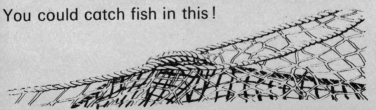

pe

penguins

more words to say
pebbles, pen, petals, pelican,
pendulum, peg, pest, peck

What is this . . .   and this?

re

record

more words to say
rest, rent, relative, restaurant,
rescue, referee

What colour is this?

se

sentry

more words to say
secretary, set, send, sell, sense

What number is this?

7

He didn't come first,
he came - - - - - .

2ⁿᵈ

te

television

more words to say
test, terrible, tell, temper, tender

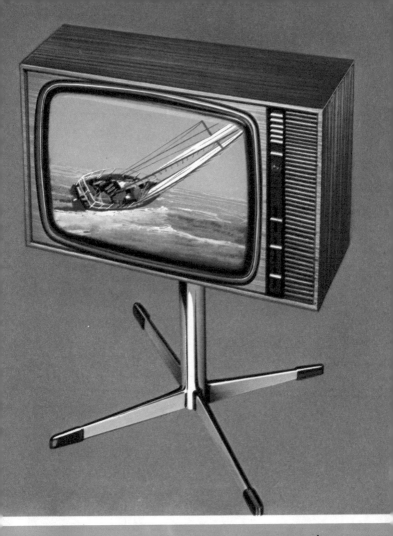

Can you name these?

10

ve

vegetables

more words to say
velvet, very, vessel, ventilator

You wear this . . .

this man cures your pet.

we

web

more words to say
wet, went, weld, Welsh, welfare

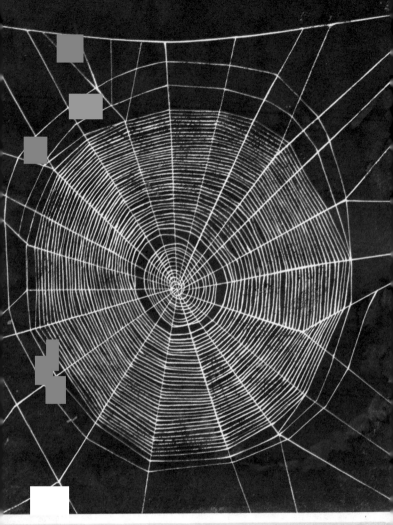

The wind is blowing from the − − − −
but the water is in the
− − − −.

ye

yellow

more words to say
yet, yesterday, yes

ze

zebra

more words to say
zenith, zest, zeppelin

ej

ejecting

more words to say
enough, evicted, enormous

What is happening here?

VOTE FOR BLOGGS

be

behind

beside

between

below

The boat is **behind** the ball

The car is **beside** the ball

The ball is **between** the car and the doll

The books are **below** the toys

Look and wait be ———— you cross.

De

December

more words to say
design, decide, defend, deserve,
deliver, delighted

ge

genie

more words to say
gene, genius, genial

December

7	14	21	28
8	15	22	29
9	16	23	30
10	17	24	31
11	18	25	
		26	

ke

keys

more words to say
keep, keen, keel

le

lever

more words to say
leek, legal, legion

me

meter
(parking meter)

more words to say
meek, meteor, meet

Pe

Peter

more words to say
peep, peel, peek

re

reflection

more words to say
repair, repeat, return, result,
remember, relations

Can you play this?

ze

zero